The World's Greatest
Brain Bogglers

The World's Greatest
Brain Bogglers

An exciting collection of crosswords, word searches, picture graphs, logic puzzles, riddles, games, and mazes—from the pages of CREATIVE KIDS magazine!

Prufrock Press Inc.
P.O. Box 8813
Waco, TX 76714-8813
Phone: (800) 998-2208
Fax: (800) 240-0333
http://www.prufrock.com

Contents

Introduction

Welcome to *The World's Greatest Brain Bogglers.* Inside the following pages, you will find challenging logic puzzles, games, word searches, crosswords, picture graphs, riddles, and mazes—all created by kids. The activities in this book were collected from the pages of *Creative Kids Magazine—The National Voice for Kids,* a magazine by and for kids ages 8-14 that contains, stories, poetry, artwork, games, photography, puzzles, and opinion.

I hope this book brings you countless hours of enjoyment and entertainment. Also, maybe it will motivate you to think up some games of your own. I challenge you to create a game or puzzle and take a chance on getting it published. Your invitation to submit work to *Creative Kids* can be found on page 61.

When this project began, it seemed to be an impossible task, but now that it's complete it feels like a triumph. These games may have the same effect on you. But like me, with a little determination and a lot of patience, you too can triumph over these brain boggling challenges. So, get ready, set, and enjoy!

—Libby Lindsey

Number Puzzle

Fill in the blanks with the numbers 3 and 5. Each row and column must equal to 21.

3				5
		3		
5				5

Donny Miller
Oak Brook, IL

Brain Boggler

My first letter is in dog but not in frog.
My sixth letter is in fin but not in fun.
My second letter is in log but not in fling.
My seventh letter is in dinner but not in digger.
My third letter is in long but not in wrong.
My fifth letter is in thing but not in string.
My fourth letter is in pond but not in fond.
What am I?

Brandon Wilson
Midland, TX

Galaxy Game

Using the ten dots, connect four in a row five times without lifting your pencil.

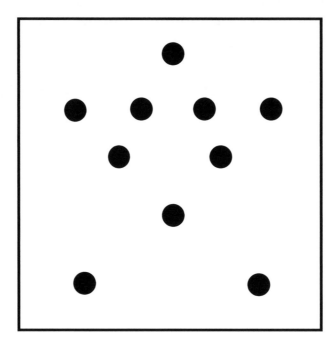

David Charpentier
West Allis, WI

Chain Link

Write a word in the space next to the clue. The last two letters of each word are the first two letters of the following word.

1. Something that erupts   _ _ _ _ _ _ _
2. _____, South, East, West   _ _ _ _ _
3. The chair of a king   _ _ _ _ _ _
4. Not old   _ _ _
5. A female sheep   _ _ _
6. Snow, hail, rain, sunshine   _ _ _ _ _ _ _
7. To wipe out   _ _ _ _ _
8. Oceans   _ _ _ _
9. To question   _ _ _
10. A short board with wheels   _ _ _ _ _ _ _ _ _

Travis Vignali
Menasha, WI

Making Connections

What is the word that comes before or after each of the three words in each group to make a compound word or a common two-word phrase?

1.	room	tub	mat	_____
2.	fall	park	lily	_____
3.	ice	soda	lolli	_____
4.	skate	hockey	berg	_____
5.	bath	bed	living	_____
6.	bow	coat	forest	_____
7.	base	basket	foot	_____
8.	hair	blow	air	_____
9.	stop	knob	hinge	_____
10.	milk	mail	post	_____

Jacque Jackson
Midland, TX

Hidden Places

In every sentence, there is a name of a country or state hidden in the words. Find the name and underline it.

Example: "The <u>unit," Ed states</u>, "is science."

1. When we went hiking, we took a mug and a backpack.
2. A large or giant animal was the least of our worries.
3. We saw a cub and a turtle on our trip.
4. Leopards are scarce, but that kind of animal, I have seen before.
5. Is that guy an animal?
6. Tom's pain in his back prevented him from going to the woods.
7. We went to the beach in a boat.
8. We were washing tons of clothes when we returned from the beach.
9. In Diana's car, I found the keys that we thought were lost.

Caitlin Peterson
Castleton, NY

Pictures Worth A Thousand Words

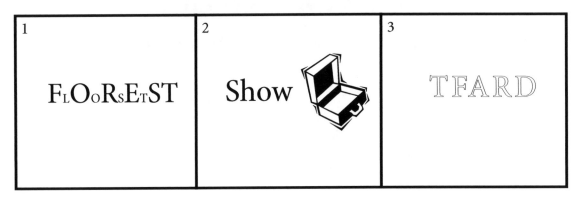

Kayla Cochran, Thomas Teets, and Nathan Cogar, Arthurdale, WV

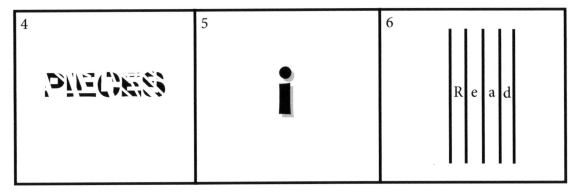

Maggie Acuna and Sarah Gitelis, Oak Brook, IL

7	8	9
poppd	ↄ Future	Spring ⅡɐℲ

Stephanie Harrell, Hendersonville, TN

Ad Lib

Find a friend and ask him or her to give you:

1. girl's name
2. noun
3. holiday
4. adjective ending in est

5. place
6. adjective
7. verb
8. adjective

9. store
10. number
11. boy's name

Write the words your friend gives you on the assigned spaces. Read back the story to your friends and get ready to laugh!

Dear Aunt _____ ,
　　　　　　　　girl's name

　　　Thank you for the _____ that you got me for _____ . It must be the _____
　　　　　　　　　　　　　　noun　　　　　　　　　　　　　　　holiday　　　　　　　　　　adjective ending in est

present in _____ ! It is so _____ ! I've never had a toy that could _____ . All
　　　　　　place　　　　　　　　　adjective　　　　　　　　　　　　　　　　　　　　　　verb

the kids in school have this _____ toy. I bet that you bought it at _____ . I've seen _____
　　　　　　　　　　　　　　adjective　　　　　　　　　　　　　　　　　　　store　　　　　　　　　　number

commercials on it. Thank you again.

　　　　　　　　　　　　　　　　　　　　　Your nephew,

　　　　　　　　　　　　　　　　　　　　　_____
　　　　　　　　　　　　　　　　　　　　　boy's name

Jacquelyn S. Hatch
Utica, OH

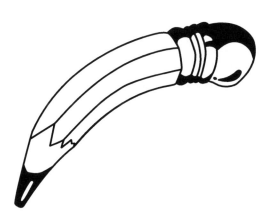

Brain Boggler

On January 1, a girl said to a boy, "Two days ago, I was 7, but next year I'll be 10." She was telling the truth. Try to figure out how this could be possible.

Pamela Massey
San Antonio, TX

Scrambled States

Use the clues to discover the state names.

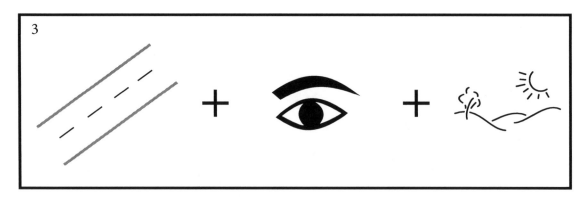

Nithya Vaduganathan, Houston, TX

On the Job

Jessica Dunn
Sugar Land, TX

Five girls were planning to get together on Friday night for a party. Each said that she would come if no other plans came up. By some coincidence, however, all five of them received calls for babysitting jobs that night. None of them had much money, therefore, all five girls chose to babysit. Each girl went to a different residence and played a different game. Each of them also watched a different movie and ate a different snack. Using the clues, determine the residence each girl went to, the movie each watched, the game each played, and the snack each ate?

1. Brenda didn't watch a movie with her first initial in its name. She babysat for the Saphins once, but they never called again.

2. Either Laura or Rachel went to the Dunhi residence; the other played *Aggravation*. Emily either played checkers or went to the Davis residence.

3. The girl who played *Aggravation* went to the Alrich residence. The girl who went to the Nebori residence either played *Life* or checkers. The girl who played checkers didn't babysit for a family starting with the letter D.

4. Emily played either checkers or *Sorry!* The girl who ate chips was either Brenda or Emily.

5. The girl at the Davis house watched either *The Secret Garden* or *Sleepless in Seattle*. Laura ate either popcorn or chips. Emily ate either peanuts or chips.

6. Rachel watched a Disney animated movie. The girl who ate chips doesn't like anything related to Disney.

7. Brenda doesn't like to wait for food to be prepared in the microwave. Laura is allergic to chocolate.

8. Either Rachel or Laura played *Aggravation*; the other played *Sorry!* Laura didn't watch *Aladdin*. The girl who played *Sorry!* watched *Beauty and the Beast*.

9. Emily hates animated movies because the events and characters seem fake to her.

10. The girl who watched *The Secret Garden* ate a candy bar and was either Jennifer or Laura. Brenda didn't watch a movie set in Seattle, or an animated movie.

11. Rachel's mother doesn't like her to eat any thing sweet unless it's also healthy for her.

	Alrich	Nebori	Saphin	Dunhi	Davis	Checkers	Sorry!	Clue	Life	Aggravation	Garden	Home Alone	Aladdin	Beauty	Seattle	Candy Bar	Chips	Peanuts	Cookies	Popcorn
Brenda																				
Jennifer																				
Laura																				
Rachel																				
Emily																				

Fictionaries

A fictionary is similar to a dictionary, except it contains fictional words that closely resemble real words.

Example:
_ A S K E T B A L L   A sport played only on Halloween night.
Masketball

1. Musical Instrument Fictionary:
   _ _ _ C U S S I O N   A cold drum section.

2. Dog Fictionary:
   _ _ E E P D O G   An English dog that always snoozes.

3. Pro Football Team Fictionaries:
   _ _ A M S   A team that likes to eat canned meat.
   _ _ A C K E R S   A team that likes ducks.

4. Sports Fictionaries:
   _ O O T B A L L   A game that chimney sweeps play.
   _ _ E F E R E E   An official who cooks.

Sara Busch, Andrea Kuhn, Ashley Miller, Brad Gade,
Derek Scallon, Adam Epley, and Chris Green, Waverly, IA

Brain Boggler

There are two boys who look exactly the same. They both have blonde hair and blue eyes. But they are not twins. Each boy has the same mother and was born on the same day. If they are not twins, how can this be?

Mindy Townsend
Aiken, SC

Sports Word Search

Find the sports terms. Words may be up, down, across, backward, or diagonal.

```
      H M R K C O U R T Y
      D O E C W A R K M L Y P
    Y V C V K M B O W L I N G M
    A S L K N H I J T N L O Q K Z U
  H T B U E B X Q R E Y A R N R C K J
C O Z A S Y D J A J E B B U H J T U V G
X A R U S O E G C A L L G N I M M I W S A F
B R S H K C I K R L G Y U H F K G M Y C F I
D R E L E S E F O Z M I R C E T E Z G T H E
E A R O T R J V T C S E U E F Z O N O T K L
I C I V W E O K K B C I S D H M I O L S C D
C I D E N T L P E C N K Y K O T I L F A S T
G N I P C U R D O M V S C C A R E O O N A O
W G N R F B A S E L O Q T K S T R T S M S S
    X G Y B O S I W U R W S I E H C T A C R
    Q H I W A N O A P A V B B T D N J G
      A S L N N U U R T C R A J K I O
      Z A M E N L H M X K Y Z L A
      B Y T X A Z Q I W E Y L
      G V F I S H I N G T
```

VOLLEY, BASKET, KICK, CAR RACING, JUMP, BALL, FOOT, HORSERIDING, GOAL, SWIMMING, SOCCER, RACKET, PUNT, SKI, TENNIS, MIT, TRACK, FIELD, FISHING, CATCH, SKATING, COURT, HOCKEY, BOWLING, BASE, GOLF, BIKE

Eric A. Fultz
Midland, TX

Brain Boggler

What do you call a pest's guess?

Ross Phillips
Klein, TX

United States
Maze

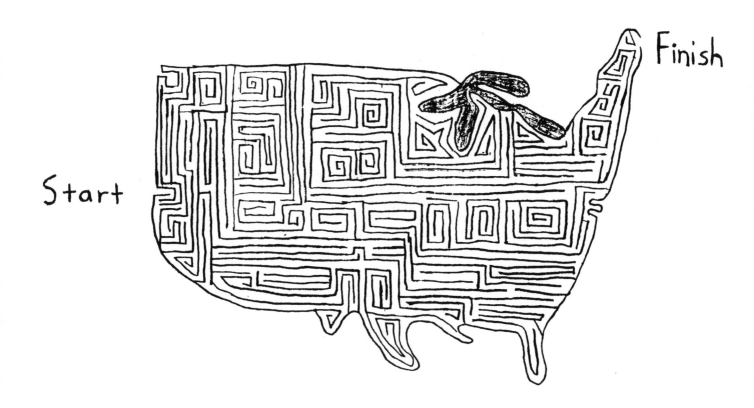

Start

Finish

Nick Petro
Midland, TX

Dr. Seuss Crossword

Use the clues to complete the puzzle.

Jeffrey Bridges
Midland, TX

ACROSS

3. His book for grandparents.
5. Seuss was a writer and an
    _____.
6. Seuss wrote books of _____.
7. Seuss won these for his movies.
9. His favorite book.
12. Seuss' last published book.
14. The person who wanted to steal Christmas.
16. Seuss' real name.

DOWN

1. Seuss is _____ for writing books.
2. He wrote scripts for his movies during this war.
4. A book about a kitty.
8. When he was 13, this began.
10. He wanted to make children _____.
11. Seuss was an illustrator and a
    _____.
13. He worked for a _____ company before he started writing books.
14. Seuss wore reading _____.
15. Dr. Seuss' first book was an
    _____.
17. _____ is his middle name.

Clock Puzzle

Draw lines connecting two numbers until all of the numbers are used. The sum of the two numbers should equal the sum of the other pairs.

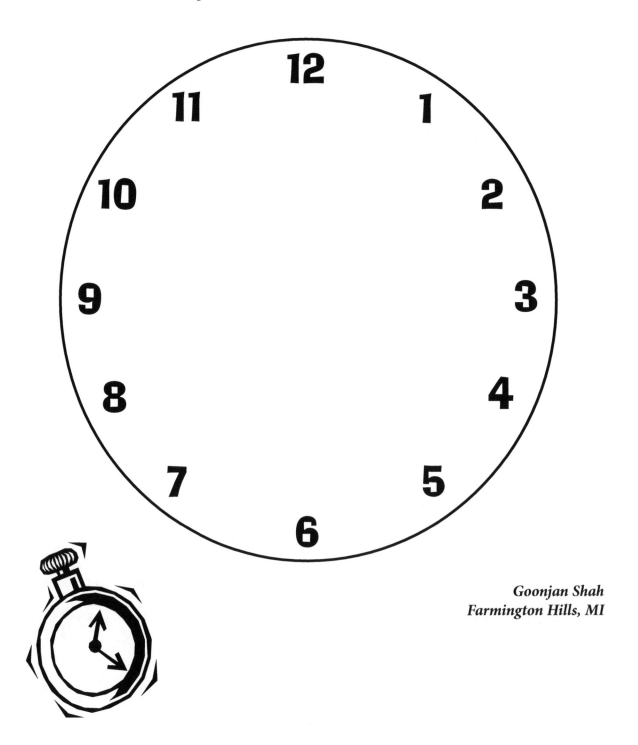

Goonjan Shah
Farmington Hills, MI

Friendly Code

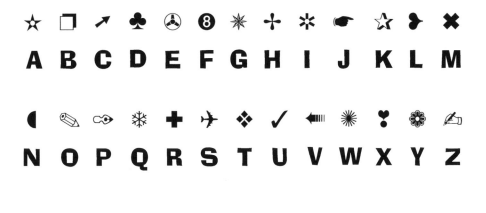

A	B	C	D	E	F	G	H	I	J	K	L	M

N	O	P	Q	R	S	T	U	V	W	X	Y	Z

Ashley Rutledge
Clarksville, TX

Puzzled About Writing

Use the clues to complete the puzzle.

ACROSS:

2. A word that expresses action.
7. A writing utensil.
9. An explanation for an article or illustration.
11. To repeat a passage or statement.
12. To space at the beginning of a paragraph from the regular margin.
15. A story or an account.
16. A person, place, or thing.

DOWN:

1. Material used to write on.
3. A word that expresses strong emotion.
4. A mark of punctuation which indicates a pause in the sentence.
5. Punctuation used after the greeting of a letter.
6. To begin a word with a capital letter.
8. A "modern age" thinking machine that performs rapid calculations and compiles data.
9. A word that connects words, phrases, or clauses.
10. Standardized marks used in sentences.
13. A book of words with definitions and pronunciations.
14. A writing machine that reproduces letters that resemble printed ones.

Jack Sisson
Oak Brook, IL

Making Monsters

A few creative (but forgetful) doctors invented some new monsters. Dr. Drathimer, Dr. Fariche, Dr. Duehicel, and Dr. Nartor made the Wachen, the Zart, the Fariche Monster, and the Trassey. When the doctors came in the next day they had forgotten who had created which monster. Use the clues to determine who invented which monster.

1. Someone whose last name begins with a D made the Zart.
2. Dr. Fariche always names his inventions after himself.
3. The Zart isn't tame and often roars.
4. Dr. Drathimer likes quiet.
5. Dr. Nartor is very disorganized.
6. The Trassey is a very messy monster.

	Wachen	Zart	Fariche Monster	Trassey
Dr. Drathimer				
Dr. Fariche				
Dr. Duehicel				
Dr. Nartor				

Alex Munter
Yardley, PA

Chain Reaction

Write a compound word in the space next to the clue. The last syllable of each word is the first syllable of the following word.

1. The schedule before a space shuttle takes off. __ __ __ __ __ __ __ __ __
2. The direction toward the bottom of a slope. __ __ __ __ __ __ __ __
3. Part of a slope. __ __ __ __ __ __ __
4. A small performance apart from the main one. __ __ __ __ __ __ __
5. A glass display used in stores. __ __ __ __ __ __ __
6. A situation in which guidance is given. __ __ __ __ __ __ __
7. A room or building where work is done. __ __ __ __ __ __ __
8. Dirty from being displayed in a store. __ __ __ __ __ __ __
9. Used until it is no longer useful. __ __ __ __ __ __
10. Playing area beyond the infield. __ __ __ __ __ __ __
11. A type of rock used in building. __ __ __ __ __ __ __ __
12. A heavy type of pottery that contains sand. __ __ __ __ __ __ __ __
13. A building where goods are stored. __ __ __ __ __ __ __ __
14. A two-winged insect found around houses. __ __ __ __ __ __ __
15. A part on a machine that regulates speed. __ __ __ __ __ __ __
16. An aid used by people who are unable to walk. __ __ __ __ __ __ __ __ __
17. A line of seats used to carry skiers up a slope. __ __ __ __ __ __ __ __ __
18. The sudden upward movement of a spacecraft. __ __ __ __ __ __ __

Tad Kimball
Merrimack, NH

Brain Boggler

What do you have when you are sitting down that disappears when you stand up?

Lindsay Lingerman
Baltimore, MD

Hinky Pinkies

Fill in the blanks with rhyming words that fit the definitions.

1. A mean father _____
2. A fat dog _____
3. A rad farm animal _____
4. A woozy critter _____
5. Wonderful fish food _____
6. A small hot dog _____
7. A bashful man _____
8. A frightening fruit _____
9. Metal fungi _____
10. An alligator grin _____
11. A cruel vegetable _____
12. Tasty steak _____
13. Good fruit _____
14. A mutt milk cap _____
15. An imitation ice cream drink _____

Adam Clark and Jimmy Keenan
Phoenix, AZ

Brain Boggler

You are selling a bike and one person offers you $735 and another person offers you $7,000, but you refuse both offers. Then, the two people get together and offer you the sum of their money. What should you do?

Add the two amounts on a calculator. Turn the calculator over and see what you should do.

Nathan True
Danville, KY

Pictures Worth A Thousand Words

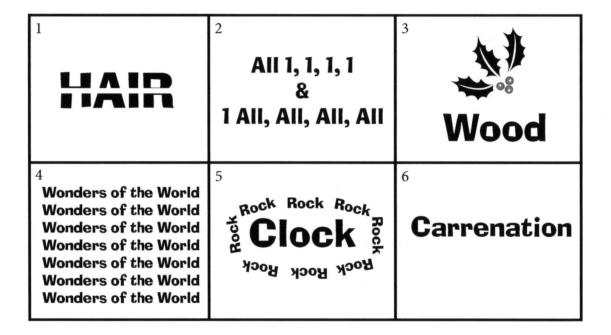

Gina Erickson and Jessica Ruttan
Phoenix, AZ

Brain Boggler

What do you call it when a dog talks?

Brent C. Paige
Houston, TX

School Days
Word Search

Find the school terms. Words may be up, down, across, backward, or diagonal.

```
M H E B I T Z C O M P U T E R S A A G R D
N Q U X U E H H L E A R N I N G B U M D H
Q Y K I D S R A B A C K P A C K C R U J S
X B A D I T R L Y U S C I E N C E E S L D
Y T F L L S J K J C I S J A M K Y J I S R
A Y G K S S D B K Y H K R G C W E C C E E
W N A N L C L O C K O A P O B J N R S Y W
E G E N U D O A V O A V L Z O E Q A G O Y
E P R I N T E R B W N G N K P M R Y D V U
K Q A S C D E D U C A T I O N E D O M K S
E U F P H S L E I L Y J V B T B F N Z D B
N O I S E R F S F C L A S S P E T S N E I
D R H N O R L K A R T P K M L L B E Q Z N
S N O W D A Y S G G X I L O A L I O U W D
O G S Q K R T H O M E W O R K R H D O Z E
X F Y C B E M Q N U C H N N F T K W B K R
H O Q D E I T B R H C G T E A C H E R S S
H U D F Q O H E O S E G Y M W R Q D R K H
V E T X Y M F J D G S K E V G F Y S O S B
```

DICTIONARY   CHALKBOARD   WORLD BOOK
CLASS PET   EDUCATION   COMPUTERS
CLASSROOM   NOTEBOOKS   SNOW DAYS
WEEKENDS   LEARNING   BACKPACK
HOMEWORK   TEACHERS   CRAYONS
MARKERS   SCIENCE   ENGLISH
PRINTER   FRIENDS   BINDERS
PENCILS   ERASER   SCHOOL
LOCKER   NOISE   CHALK
CLOCK   DESKS   MUSIC
LUNCH   PAPER   TESTS
MATH   FLAG   KIDS
BELL   PENS   ART
BUS   GYM

Katie Fabio and Jennifer Hill
Wantagh, NY

Hidden Animals

Find the animal hidden in each of the following sentences.

1. Tobacco will cause cancer.
2. Fifi shied away from the other dog.
3. Mom likes to read eerie books.
4. The man's business was called, Lemmon Keys & Locks.
5. If the pump ignites, will it explode?
6. Did you win at the clam bake?
7. Joey Schmoo severely injured his arm when he fell.
8. Maybe Arthur would like a piece of cake.

Joey Heller
Phoenix, AZ

Chain Link

Write a word in the space next to the clue. The last two letters of each word are the first two letters of the following word.

1. A dark color _ _ _ _ _ _ _
2. Leafy vegetable _ _ _ _ _ _ _ _
3. A point within a circle _ _ _ _ _ _ _
4. Being worn away gradually _ _ _ _ _ _ _ _
5. Sometimes put on hot dogs _ _ _ _ _ _
6. First word in a lot of fairy tales _ _ _ _
7. In or near the center _ _ _ _ _ _ _ _
8. Short for Alexander _ _ _ _
9. More than usual _ _ _ _ _
10. A baby's toy _ _ _ _ _ _

Kari Ehlke
Menasha, WI

Where in the World?

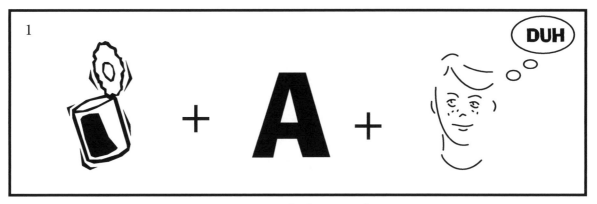

Aaron Zulaski, Des Plains, IL

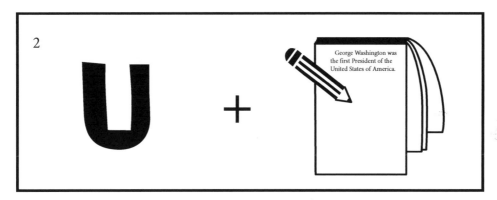

A.J. Watson, Des Plaines, IL

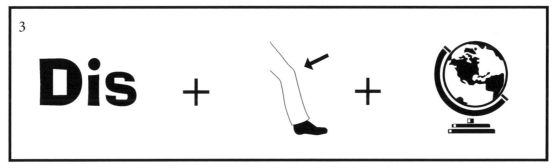

Katie Byrne, Des Plaines, IL

Man Maze

Chris Murphy
Ithaca, NY

Brain Boggler

It cannot be seen, it cannot be felt. It cannot be heard, it cannot be smelt. It lies behind stars and under hills, and empty holes it always fills. It comes first and follows after. What is it?

Jeni Borth
Plains, KS

Making Connections

What is the word that comes before or after each of the three words in each group to make a compound word or a common two-word phrase?

1. hog	crew	floor	_____
2. air	ache	board	_____
3. lace	line	tie	_____
4. pump	mail	line	_____
5. bow	cut	raising	_____
6. mate	shape	friend	_____
7. fill	slide	mark	_____
8. yard	room	martial	_____
9. wife	work	ware	_____
10. shake	saw	made	_____
11. room	rock	flower	_____
12. whirl	car	swimming	_____
13. man	glue	bowl	_____
14. coat	done	cooked	_____
15. knuckle	park	room	_____
16. day	reading	weight	_____
17. night	dressing	top	_____
18. black	head	clip	_____
19. struck	beam	rock	_____
20. pad	cap	high	_____

Jared Allison, Robert Coleman, Lance Cottle, Jennifer Dampier, Vicki Gaskins, Zachariah Huddleston, Lacy Jackson, Jenny Preston, and Jarrod Whitfield, Lake City, FL

Brain Boggler

Where do rabbits go to rollerskate?

Marion Brant
Klein, TX

The Great Bike Race

Six people held a bike race. Their names were Mark, Ed, Sean, Julia, Amy, and Diane. The colors of their bikes were red, white, yellow, green, blue, and black. Their bikes were also numbered 1-6. They won first, second, third, fourth, fifth, and sixth place. See if you can figure out who won what place and what number and color each of their bikes were. Use the clues below.

1. Sean finished before number 3 and after Amy.
2. The yellow bike was the fastest, but fell over and ended up in fourth place.
3. Number 6 bike came in first.
4. Number 4's black bike was the slowest.
5. Amy doesn't like black or white.
6. Number 3 finished in fifth place.
7. Number 2 was a red bike.
8. Diane won the race with her green bike.
9. Number 5 bike belonged to a boy.
10. Amy was number 2.
11. Mark likes to tease Ed because he thinks Ed's white bike is plain.
12. Now, Ed teases Mark because Mark came in fifth place.
13. Diane dislikes black and yellow.
14. Everything Sean owns is yellow.
15. Number 2 came in third after number 5.
16. Ed came in second place.
17. The yellow bike had the number 1 on it.
18. The blue bike was faster than the black bike.
19. Julia was number 4.

Jill Johnson
Lewisville, TX

Pig Trivia

Use the symbols to fill in the blanks below.

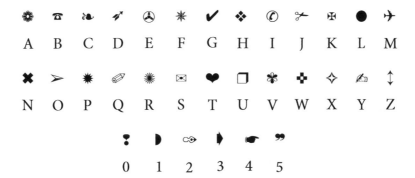

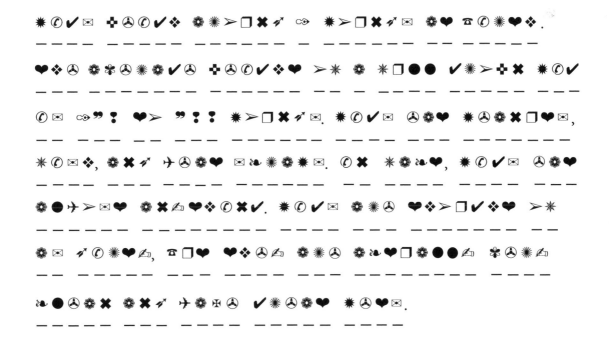

Isabel Alvarado
Midland, TX

Volleyball
Word Search
**Find the volleyball terms. Words may be
up, down, across, backward, or diagonal.**

```
V  D  S  E  R  V  E  H  P  M  B  F  H  S  S  F
M  O  X  C  D  F  H  K  L  T  U  K  D  S  O  L
B  O  L  O  K  C  M  N  V  S  S  X  C  O  L  K
Q  W  B  L  O  C  K  C  V  B  E  D  T  F  F  L
B  A  S  T  E  M  F  U  R  E  T  F  M  K  L  N
U  S  A  K  U  Y  D  E  Q  A  A  I  J  K  G  H
M  A  I  S  V  X  B  V  D  U  S  F  G  C  R  E
P  P  H  Y  W  R  T  A  L  I  G  D  R  A  O  P
S  G  K  L  D  E  A  T  L  W  A  B  N  T  P  Q
P  S  T  G  B  V  Z  N  P  L  M  A  W  T  P  L
A  X  C  V  F  D  E  E  L  K  G  F  S  A  G  S
V  F  S  A  W  R  F  T  A  Q  D  G  T  T  Y  U
K  N  E  E  P  A  D  S  D  H  D  H  C  A  E  B
A  F  H  T  F  E  D  S  H  J  E  S  F  H  J  D
S  F  G  H  F  F  D  A  H  R  E  D  F  Y  U  R
T  R  U  O  C  O  M  P  E  T  I  T  I  O  N  S
```

VOLLEYBALL, SET, BEACH, SERVE, KNEEPADS, COURT, PASS,
FOOTFAULT, COMPETITION, BLOCK, NET, ATTACK, BUMP, SPIKE

Cara Barger
Portland, IN

Brain Boggler

Grandma likes records, but not tapes. She likes
swimming, but not water. She prefers glue to tape.
She loves coffee, but hates tea. She likes wood, but
not trees. What *one* thing does grandma dislike the
most?

Heidi Hockett
Boone, IA

Concealed Fruit

In every sentence, there is a name of a fruit hidden in the words. Find the name and underline it.

Example: Chea**p lum**ber is hard to find.

1. Could you give me my cap, please?
2. Papa, pay a dollar to the milkman.
3. "Make the hog rap!" Einstein said.
4. The big dog Fido ran gently toward the fence.
5. The pea changed color during the summer.
6. Play the tuba, Nan, as loud as you can.

Julia and Robert Knox
Richmond, VA

Hinky Pinkies

Fill in the blanks with rhyming words that fit the definitions.

1. A cat's gloves _____
2. A fire-breathing automobile _____
3. A counterfeit garden tool _____
4. A bug dessert _____
5. An insect drink _____
6. A whispering protest _____
7. A weasel's vegetables _____
8. A calf's food _____
9. A weird ape _____
10. A caterpillar's movement _____
11. A big boat _____
12. An important pachyderm _____
13. Grizzly fur _____
14 A weird hawk _____
15. A high shopping center _____

Chris Gawad, Ian Kushner, Joey Nuara,
and Kip Shearer, Phoenix, AZ

Authors & Movie Stars Crossword

Use the clues to complete the puzzle.

ACROSS:

1. She says, "My, what big teeth you have."
4. He is the producer of the TV show *ER*.
5. She wrote *Lassie*.
6. The author of *Windcatcher* is _____.
7. He plays Ray in the *Ghostbuster* movies.
10. He directed *Schlinder's List*.
12. He was bitten in the movie *Wolf*.
13. He is Captain Kirk in the *Star Trek* movie.
14. She played the mom in *Mrs. Doubtfire*.

DOWN:

2. He played Dr. Kimble in *The Fugitive*.
3. He was Peter Pan in the movie *Hook*.
5. He is the director of the movie *E.T.*
8. He is the author of *The Hardy Boys*.
9. He is the author of *The Goosebumps Series*.
11. He played *Forrest Gump*.

Scott Kniaz and Andy Labanauskas
Oak Brook, IL

Dream Team I Word Search

Find the names of basketball players. Words may be up, down, across, or backward.

```
M  I  C  H  A  E  L  J  O  R  D  A  N  P  C
N  E  P  P  I  P  E  I  T  T  O  C  S  A  H
C  R  F  C  L  A  E  T  T  N  E  R  J  T  A
H  E  T  R  S  K  B  D  L  V  G  N  O  R  R
R  N  Y  L  A  W  Q  N  Z  X  C  V  H  I  L
I  O  B  N  M  A  S  D  F  G  H  J  N  C  E
S  L  K  L  Q  W  E  R  P  T  Y  U  S  K  S
M  A  G  I  C  J  O  H  N  S  O  N  T  E  B
U  M  D  H  K  S  P  V  C  L  F  I  O  W  A
L  L  U  L  A  R  R  Y  B  I  R  D  C  I  R
I  R  L  M  F  N  E  H  L  K  V  S  K  N  K
I  A  P  U  T  W  G  J  B  X  Q  P  E  G  L
N  K  Y  E  R  T  U  V  K  L  E  S  N  E  E
D  A  V  I  D  R  O  B  I  N  S  O  N  W  Y
C  L  Y  D  E  D  R  E  X  L  E  R  G  B  Y
```

Karl Malone, Scottie Pippen, Larry Bird, Michael Jordan, C. Laettner, Chris Mullin, Patrick Ewing, David Robinson, Magic Johnson, Charles Barkley, Clyde Drexler, John Stocken

Michael Rager
Portland, IN

Brain Boggler

What can make someone throw a temper tantrum, be in a bad mood, be happy and cheerful, hold him or her in suspense, and break his or her heart all at the same time?

Craig Bailey
Geneva, IN

Pictures Worth A Thousand Words

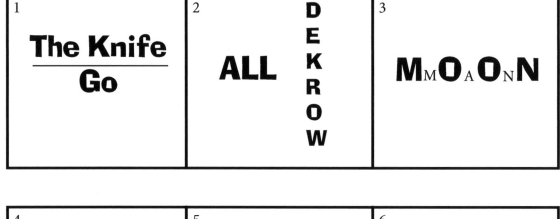

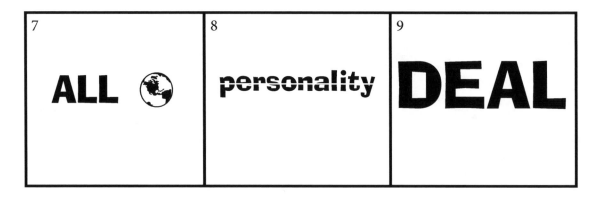

Danielle and Jessica Dunn, Sugar Land, TX

Pastimes

The scrambled clues are fun things to do indoors and out. When you finish, read the shaded column to reveal a message.

1. EVMSIO
2. YCNILBGIC
3. NRTGAFI
4. HKARSEBOC NDGIIR
5. LYELOBLVAL
6. OHCEYK
7. RGDAINW
8. IKGNHI
9. AGNNTIPI
10. CDEAN
11. GNKTASI
12. HGSINIF
13. IODVE GESMA
14. ADGIENR
15. YSTSCNGAMI
16. SMCUI

Stephanie Evans
Yakima, WA

Chain Link

Write a word in the space next to the clue. The last two letters of each word are the first two letters of the following word.

1. The planet on which we live   _ _ _ _ _
2. Used to measure temperature   _ _ _ _ _ _ _ _ _ _ _
3. A mistake   _ _ _ _ _
4. A citrus fruit   _ _ _ _ _ _
5. A country in north central Europe   _ _ _ _ _ _ _
6. A strong, synthetic material   _ _ _ _ _
7. _____, two, three   _ _ _
8. Used to sew   _ _ _ _ _ _
9. A stick of graphite, used in pencils   _ _ _ _
10. To counsel   _ _ _ _ _ _

Emily Rowan
Midland, TX

Magic Squares

Make every line, vertical, horizontal, and diagonal, equal 15 using addition. Only use the numbers 1-9 one time each.

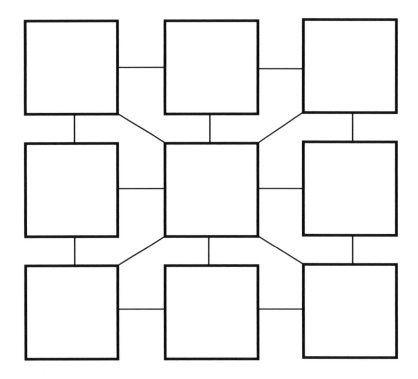

Rahul Sawlani
Oak Brook, IL

Brain Boggler

What stops every minute and goes on everyday? What can be given or taken away? What comes with chance and is a comrade of time? What is as soft as a flower and sharp as a knife?

Ed Strietelmeir
Portland, IN

Movie Titles Crossword

Use the clues to complete the puzzle.

ACROSS:
1. To go very fast.
4. "Eat me. Drink me."
6. Small females.
10. Very large.
11. It covers your face.
12. Unclean polka.
13. No one is in the house but you.

DOWN:
2. _____, Pennsylvania
3. He said, "Stupid is as stupid does."
5. He wanted to phone home.
7. He was running from the law.
8. An indecent weapon.
9. An unintelligent elephant.

Karly Savara
Rockford, MI

35

Hidden Names

Find the last names of professional basketball players hidden in the sentences.

1. John's on the phone, do you want to talk to him?
2. The man's name is Major Dan Jones.
3. Stop kidding around, Fred.
4. One Alka-Seltzer, please.
5. Why doesn't the dog bark, Leya?

Zack Geist and J.D. Tate
Phoenix, AZ

Chain Link

Write a word in the space next to the clue. The last two letters of each word are the first two letters of the following word.

1. A particular person or thing   _ _ _
2. Part of the body containing the brain   _ _ _ _
3. Opposite of subtraction   _ _ _ _ _ _ _ _
4. A single thing   _ _ _
5. Clean and tidy   _ _ _ _
6. The past tense of eat   _ _ _
7. Plural of tooth   _ _ _ _ _
8. To toss   _ _ _ _ _
9. To be indebted for   _ _ _
10. To cry   _ _ _ _

Jonelle Trader
Menasha, WI

Sports Match

There were 5 girls and boys who went to Duncan County Middle School. They each played a different sport. Use the clues to help match their first and last names, and the sports they played.

1. Andy and Smith both like to play with bouncy balls but Andy hits his ball with a racket.
2. Leslie cheers for Tori and Giddens.
3. Michelle's father is John Jones.
4. Tori's family owns Smith Jewelers.
5. Moore can jump very high.
6. Cheerleaders are only at football and basketball games.
7. The boys are Andy and Jamie.

	Andy	Michelle	Tori	Jamie	Leslie	Cheerleader	Tennis	Baseball	Basketball	Football
Giddens										
Moore										
Parker										
Jones										
Smith										

Katie Morrison
Eastman, GA

Brain Boggler

What tune does a skunk play on a piano?

Micah McCombs
Spring, TX

Crazy Maze

*Josh Banks
Newark, OH*

Picture Graph

Plot the following list of ordered pairs. The first number is the horizontal number on the graph, and the second number is the vertical number. Connect the dots along the way until you come to the word STOP, then lift your pencil. Begin with the next group of numbers and connect them as you go. Complete column one before moving on to column two, and so on.

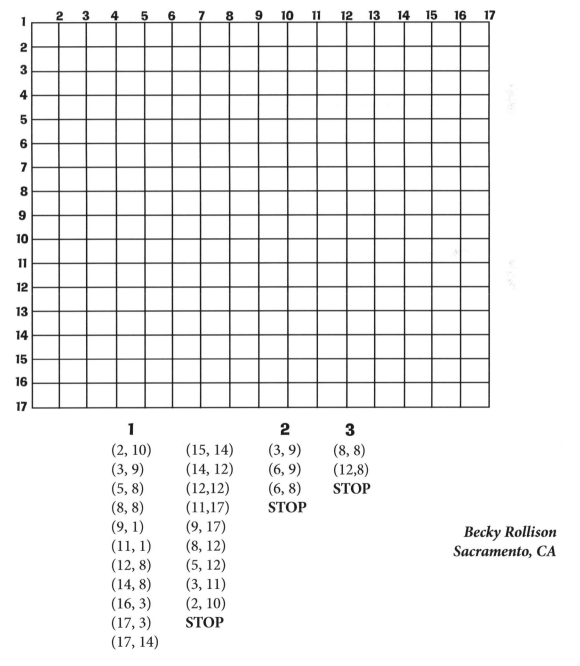

1		2	3
(2, 10)	(15, 14)	(3, 9)	(8, 8)
(3, 9)	(14, 12)	(6, 9)	(12,8)
(5, 8)	(12,12)	(6, 8)	**STOP**
(8, 8)	(11,17)	**STOP**	
(9, 1)	(9, 17)		
(11, 1)	(8, 12)		
(12, 8)	(5, 12)		
(14, 8)	(3, 11)		
(16, 3)	(2, 10)		
(17, 3)	**STOP**		
(17, 14)			

Becky Rollison
Sacramento, CA

Eagle Trivia

Use the symbols to fill in the blanks below.

A B C D E F G H I J K L M

N O P Q R S T U V W X Y Z

___ ___ ___ ___ ___   ___ ___ ___ ___ ___ ___   ___ ___ ___   ___ ___ ___ ___ ___   ___ ___ ___ ___   ___ ___ ___ ___

___ ___ ___ ___ ___ ___   ___ ___ ___ ___ ___ ___   ___ ___ ___ ___ ___ ___   ___ ___   ___ ___ ___ ___   ___ ___ ___   ___ ___   ___ ___ ___   ___ ___ ___ ___

___ ___   ___ ___ ___ ___ ___ ___ ___   ___ ___ ___   ___ ___ ___ ___ ___ ___ ___,   ___ ___ ___ ___   ___ ___ ___   ___ ___ ___ ___ ___ ___ ___

___ ___ ___ ___ ___ ___ ___   ___ ___   ___ ___ ___ ___ ___ ___ ___.   ___ ___ ___ ___ ___   ___ ___ ___ ___ ___   ___ ___ ___ ___ ___   ___ ___   ___ ___ ___ ___,

___ ___ ___   ___ ___ ___ ___   ___ ___ ___ ___ ___   ___ ___ ___ ___ ___ ___   ___ ___   ___ ___ ___ ___ ___ ___ ___   ___ ___ ___ ___ ___ .

___ ___ ___ ___   ___ ___ ___ ___ ___ ___ ___   ___ ___ ___ ___ ___   ___ ___ ___ ___   ___ ___ ___ ___ ___ ___ ___ ___   ___ ___   ___ ___ ___

___ ___ ___ ___ ___   ___ ___ ___ ___ ___   ___ ___ ___ ___ ___ ___.

Trevor Best
Midland, TX

Making Connections

What is the word that comes before or after each of the three words in each group to make a compound word or a common two-word phrase?

1. sharp	saw	baby	_____
2. handle	maid	stool	_____
3. butter	horse	house	_____
4. worm	store	mark	_____
5. sun	high	pin	_____
6. room	bugs	spread	_____
7. bell	stop	trap	_____
8. player	deck	packing	_____
9. baby's	morning	bad	_____
10. power	board	side	_____
11. crystal	out	cut	_____
12. clock	human	down	_____
13. tale	dust	tooth	_____
14. way	strip	time	_____
15. tie	lace	band	_____
16. broken	burn	cold	_____
17. acid	light	coat	_____
18. dog	line	TV	_____
19. clothes	pig	nine	_____
20. hand	link	pant	_____
21. in	Virginia	fishing	_____
22. portable	ceiling	Chinese	_____
23. gold	toss	age	_____
24. high	room	act	_____
25. silver	shell	flying	_____

Cory Bainbridge, Jariel Bortnick, Brian Burns, Jeremy Cook, Edward Comstock, Ryan Cortez, Brianne Eichler, Aaron Feign, Katie George, Krystal Judy, Matthew Lane, Trevor Lawless, Bill Mason, Mark Mobley, Adam Montagna, Jessica Morris, Kristen Nash, Donald Postway, Brian Presson, Jason Riddle James Roberts, Marcus Sapir, Josh Seymour, Leigh Ann Sigmon, Brian Sullivan, Brandon Terrell, Michele Thompsen, and Mary Walsh, Belleview, FL

Civil War
Word Search

Find the words below in the puzzle on the opposite page. Words may be up, down, across, backward, or diagonal.

SLAVERY	FORT DONELSON
LINCOLN	RICHMOND
UNION	GETTYSBURG
CONFEDERATE	DEFEAT
NURSE	TROOPS
SOLDIERS	FORT SUMTER
BULL RUN	ABE
GENERAL	STONEWALL
ROBERT LEE	SOUTH CAROLINA
SHERMAN	GEORGIA
GRANT	BATTLE
NORTH	TOBACCO
SOUTH	CABINET
CIVIL WAR	UNITED STATES
ARMY	WAR
SLAVES	MEDAL OF HONOR
STATES	ANTIETAM CREEK
BLOCKADE	FREDRIKSBURG
EAST	WILDERNESS
EMANCIPATION PROCLAMA-	FIVE FORKS
TION	BLACK CODE
BORDER	WOUNDED
SHILOH	

Shane Miller
Menasha, WI

```
M E S R U N Y W B T N U T I E R E I C R N P L Y R R O S
O S B H I Y O C C A B O T T A J L B A A M O M Z Y R E L
C G P O A W I L L I V R I A C D N W R B O E E R Y A A G
U U E R I O E K Y T O S E I S D L I E S T I E T N U K R
I T I P M A D S T O T A M E E I N E G Y N V I I E E P U
E S H E B X Y R P I N E A R V E G N V I A T L O E E D B
M E S A A U O S G O F M N I V I S T O L L O L R U L N S
B E E T C T E N I B A C A E O M I S A R O C S E P E K
L R T S S O P I I T U C I C G T A R N A L M M R O L L I
L N A A N T D K R A W E P O C A E N C R A E V E K Y Z R
A O T A H C C E F T W U A I M I D H O T N E I R Q P J D
W M S W I L D E R N E S T N D T T I E N R E C E H M N E
E P D P D R G N L O C N I L I U P I O I S D S E W O W R
N U E E M R A N L I I R O F O E T R W G N A O L I N I F
O E T H O L I H S A N S N S I N T H M E C K C T T Y R A
T R I O A H I I I R J A P E A H I T E Y I C U R O K N G
S L N Y C A R E D R O B R H L W A K L A V O O E V I A G
E N U G O W N U K U L M O M Z T O E T D I L E B L S R M
Z M E X A I G R O E G N C L O O T M T N L B E O O U Y D
M E T A R E D E F N O C L A T S C A A O W A R R B C G D
R S U W P W Y U T S P R A N S D C O B N A A C S N R S U
B L A C K C O D E Z Y G M M A B U V W X C L Y U A A C E
A N C S H E R M A N Y Z A W E H Y R A H O T T S S U H M
C O N O L K O R Q W W S T S T T M X T E T E I E R A N E
K S Y B G J A B E P V T I S A U A U Y E C A E L I D D P
S L O C H T I N O O P U O J T O O E G S S W A I O S O R
Q E U D S K C A L B T O N T N S A Y M R A O U I Y S A O
A N A A E W S I U Q I U N I O N L C L D S O U M E S E N
I O C E M R L L N R O A S N E I S A L H E A D T S O M O
B D A F I N L M S O R A L C O S N O V E S L A E B I N H
M T E N A R D J K G M R R E Y Y A B Z E A T N R I R G F
U R M E U E F E E S M T A E F E D E A C S R V I A A L O
L O K N D G L N R R E T M U S T R O F B E T R A K D E L
I F U N B H E M R I C H M O N D A D N D R O B B Y E O A
O U U D P R U D E D A C I L R O A V L N D H R A E R T D
C O A H A O T O T S D L S R E W O I E R E N S A I N R E
W R D L A U S K R O F E V I F G W G E O S N A O L E C M
```

History Revealed

Ellen, Sara, Debra, and Lisa were all friends at Locklaw Middle School. They each had a different history teacher, but at the same time, they were assigned papers to write by their teachers. Use the clues to determine the topic of their papers, the length, the teacher who assigned them, and the type of work.

1. Lisa didn't write the poem assigned by Mrs. Winston. Her topic was not World War II.
2. The teacher who uses Ms. instead of Mrs. does not have Ellen as a student.
3. The length of Sara's assignment was 16 lines. She wasn't told to write a letter.
4. One of the girls with four letters in her name has Mrs. Crips.
5. Mrs. Crips assigned poetry. Ellen didn't write a research paper.
6. A girl with an L in her name wrote a letter. The letter contained 500 words.
7. The research paper was supposed to be 3 pages. Mrs. Crips' topic was the Declaration of Independence. The paper on World War II was 3 pages long.
8. Lisa's letter to the government on the Constitution was assigned by a teacher whose name began with a P.

	Constitution	Decl of Indep.	World War II	American Rev.	Ms. Criston	Mrs. Winston	Mrs. Prally	Mrs. Crips	Research Paper	Poem	Letter	Fictional Story	3 Pages	16 Lines	2½ pages	500 Words
Ellen																
Sara																	
Debra																	
Lisa																	

Jessica Dunn
Sugar Land, TX

Picture Graph

Plot the list of ordered pairs. The letter is the horizontal point on the graph, and the number is the vertical point. Connect the dots along the way until you come to the word STOP, then lift your pencil. Begin with the next group of numbers and connect them as you go. Complete column one before moving on to column two, and so on.

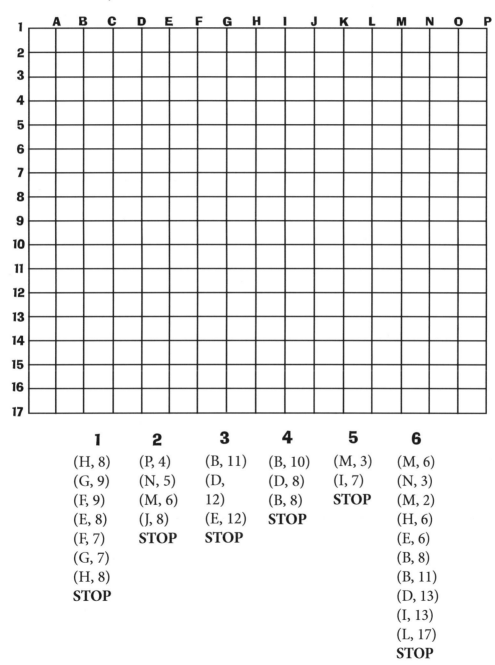

1
(H, 8)
(G, 9)
(F, 9)
(E, 8)
(F, 7)
(G, 7)
(H, 8)
STOP

2
(P, 4)
(N, 5)
(M, 6)
(J, 8)
STOP

3
(B, 11)
(D, 12)
(E, 12)
STOP

4
(B, 10)
(D, 8)
(B, 8)
STOP

5
(M, 3)
(I, 7)
STOP

6
(M, 6)
(N, 3)
(M, 2)
(H, 6)
(E, 6)
(B, 8)
(B, 11)
(D, 13)
(I, 13)
(L, 17)
STOP

Samantha Rachel
Alexandria, LA

45

Tutankhamen Crossword

Use the clues and the word list, if necessary, to complete the puzzle on the opposite page.

ACROSS

2. A word meaning hot and dry.
4. Pictures or symbols used by ancient Egyptians that represent words.
6. The 18th dynasty Egyptian king.
9. The service in which a king is crowned.
10. Tutankhamen's best friend.
12. A place where a mummy is buried.
16. Loose, gritty grains of disintegrated rock.
18. An arid country in Africa.
21. A vault or grave for the dead.
23. A large river running through Egypt.
24. An Egyptian statue having the head of a man and the body of a lion.
26. A 3-D triangle found especially in Egypt.

DOWN

1. Shoes that fasten to the foot.
3. The man who discovered King Tut's tomb.
5. An above-the-ground coffin.
7. A female god.
8. A horse-drawn, two-wheeled cart used in ancient times for war.
11. King Tut was buried with a lot of it.
13. King Tut's favorite wedding present was made of this.
14. King Tut's Mummy has a deadly _____.
15. King Tut's vizier.
17. The Egyptians believed this to be the guardian of the dead.
19. An Egyptian ruler.
20. A large fierce cat.
22. An Egyptian body that has been well preserved.
25. The Roman Numeral for eighteen.

Betsy Baker
Midland, TX

Word List	
Alabaster	Khai
Anubis	Lion
Arid	Mummy
Ay	Nile
Burial Chamber	Pharaoh
Carter	Pyramid
Chariot	Sand
Coronation	Sandals
Curse	Sarcophagus
Egypt	Sphinx
Goddess	Tomb
Gold	Tutankhamen
Hieroglyphics	XVIII

Pictures Worth a Thousand Words

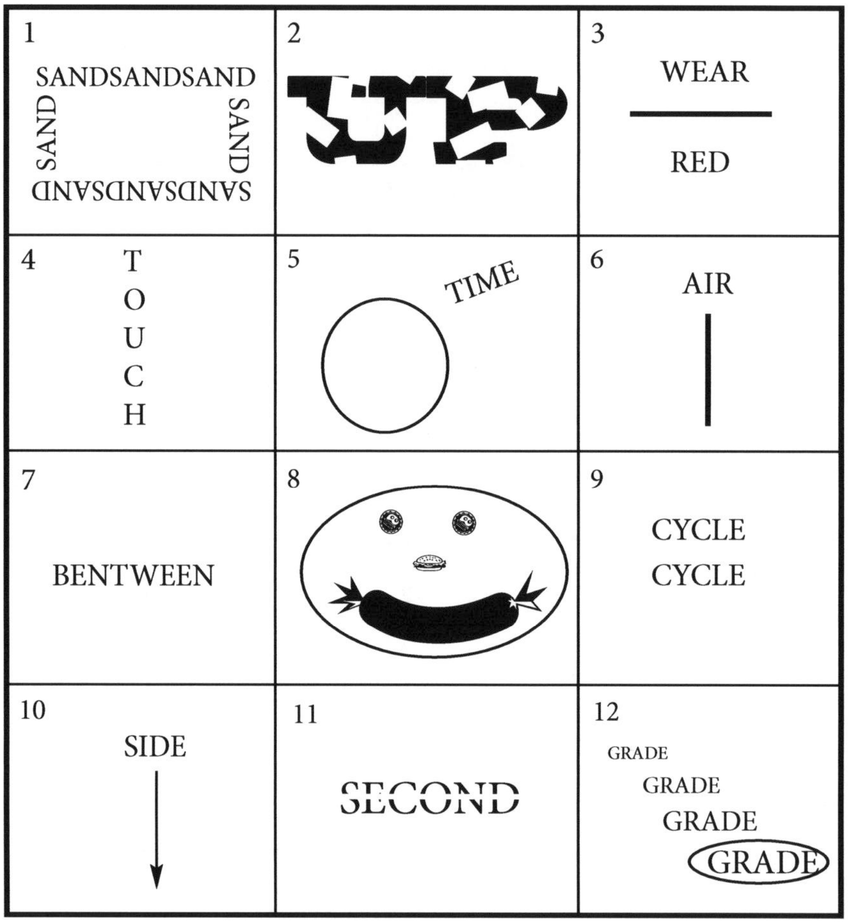

1 SANDSANDSAND SAND (with SAND on all four sides, forming a box)	2 (scrambled letters)	3 WEAR ――――― RED
4 T O U C H	5 (circle) TIME	6 AIR │
7 BENTWEEN	8 (smiley face)	9 CYCLE CYCLE
10 SIDE ↓	11 SECOND	12 GRADE GRADE GRADE (GRADE)

Jordan Blake
Katy, TX

Brain Boggler

What do you call a fish with two knees?

Allyson Holmes
Teague, TX

Chain Link

Write a word in the space next to the clue. The last two letters of each word are the first two letters of the following word.

1. It keeps you dry   _ _ _ _ _ _ _ _
2. A narrow path   _ _ _ _
3. A state   _ _ _ _ _ _ _ _
4. A cabbage   _ _ _ _
5. To go away   _ _ _ _ _
6. Small destructive animals   _ _ _ _ _ _
7. To call on   _ _ _ _ _ _
8. It's good on french fries   _ _ _ _ _ _ _
9. To disturb   _ _ _ _ _
10. A colorless liquid used as an anesthetic   _ _ _ _ _
11. To rub out   _ _ _ _ _
12. A number   _ _ _ _ _
13. The language of the people of England   _ _ _ _ _ _ _
14. To talk very loudly   _ _ _ _ _ _
15. A state   _ _ _ _
16. In front of   _ _ _ _ _
17. Ahead or higher   _ _ _ _ _ _ _ _
18. To prepare for publication   _ _ _ _
19. A bit of news or information   _ _ _ _
20. A hard, dark mineral used for grinding   _ _ _ _ _

Robby Robinson
Menasha, WI

Brain Boggler

I invented the harmonica. I had 13 brothers and sisters. I wore glasses and traveled a lot. I attended school for less than two years. I invented bifocals. I never owned a car. I flew a kite. I invented the lightning rod. I lived in Philadelphia. Who am I?

Miles Galbraith
Durango, CO

Making Connections

What is the word that comes before or after each of the three words in each group to make a compound word or a common two-word phrase?

1. day   child   health   _____
2. grass   rattle   skin   _____
3. spelling   honey   killer   _____
4. first   band   hearing   _____
5. stalk   green   brain   _____
6. fall   ski   sprinkler   _____
7. lime   gem   tomb   _____
8. bail   James   chemical   _____
9. snow   bob   dog   _____
10. bath   floor   exercise   _____

Tiffany Vargas
Midland, TX

Scrambled Phrases

Unscramble the following phrases to find clichés.

1. vreey odlcu ash a viserl nigiln
2. a idrb ni het ndha si twohr wto ni eht uhsb
3. a cttish ni imet vseas ienn
4. tdno okol a itfg hseor ni eth uhmot
5. odtn tibe hte adhn htta fsede ouy
6. egvirytehn atth acn og nrogw liwl
7. igianrn scta dan osgd
8. eehr oydat geon rwomotor
9. hreas nda asreh elkia
10. rgni dna rbae ti

Paul Hedrick
Tyler, TX

Yummy
Word Search

Find the different foods in the puzzle. Words may be up, down, across, backward, or diagonal.

```
A D E B C E P I K R N F R E N C H F R I E S
C H O K C H I C K E N P E A N U T S S K N R
D A O P K G Z C N R E A T U R K E Y H C K R
K M C P R N Z A K M Z T S Z P R N E O K R E
O B C S E E A K O N G S B A N A N A T J R I
J U K P A G O E R R K A O O C O R N D O G T
S R O I K A G N B A P P L E K E N P O R K T
R G D N D K D S U B R F E R U N S D G F K E
R E F A K N E N M B N K T G R B E A N S N H
N R O C T K N P F I S H T M A T R F N T S G
S K G H F P B D J T S I U R S T E A K V R A
C R G P U E V E S E E H C A R R O T S K C P
F M N O P G E S H U A H E E A L Y S E C R S
K H S K R J D B O L O G N A A M D T K P R D
```

PIZZA, APPLE, CAKE, LETTUCE, CARROTS, FISH, LOBSTER, CRAB, CHEESE, CHICKEN, HAMBURGER, RABBIT, SUB, BOLOGNA, BANANA, TURKEY, STEAK, BEANS, PEANUTS, PASTA, BEEF, CORNDOG, SPINACH, CORN, EGGS, HOT DOG, SPAGHETTI, PORK, SOUP, FRENCH FRIES

Josh Healy
Menasha, WI

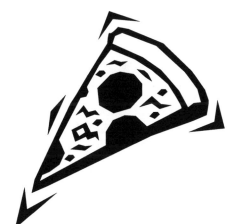

Brain Boggler

Why do grizzlies like to wear slippers?

Mark Miller
Jackson, OH

Horse Sense Crossword

Use the clues to complete the puzzle on the opposite page.

ACROSS

3. A section in a stable that a horse lives in.
4. A full-grown horse that is less than 58 inches.
5. A male horse that can be used for breeding.
7. A very useful animal.
10. A female horse that is more than four years old.
11. A wild or partly tamed horse.
13. For some, it's a hobby.
15. A seat for a rider on a horse.
16. One who rides.
19. Kentucky is popular for this sport.

DOWN

1. A horse's fastest, natural gait.
2. A u-shaped metal plate nailed to a horse's hoof.
6. A two-beat gait.
8. To climb up on something.
9. One whose job is riding horses in races.
10. A small wild horse of the southwestern plains.
12. A young horse.
14. A type of quarter horse noted for endurance.
17. Long, narrow straps attached to the bit that are. used to control the horse.
18. A ring that hangs from the saddle and is used as a footrest.

Darcee Wood
Midland, TX

Brain Boggler

My first name is George. I hit 714 home runs in my career. My uniform number is three. I was called the "Sultan of Swat." I began professional baseball at 19, and I was one of the home run kings. Who am I?

Robin Hobbs
Durango, CO

Number Puzzler

Make every line, vertical, horizontal, and diagonal, equal 9 using addition. Use the numbers 0-6. Some numbers will be used more than once.

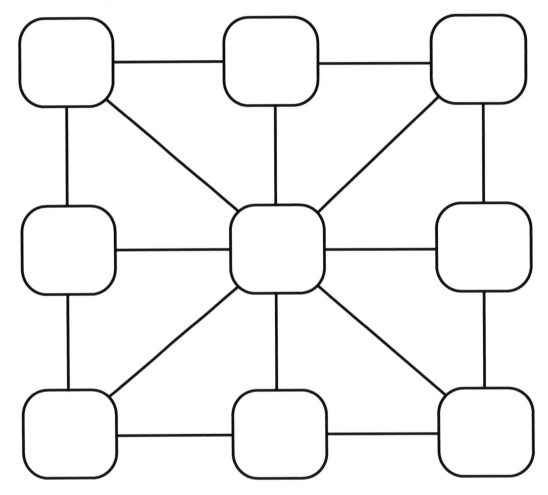

Bill Raidt and Colt Dunteman
Oak Brook, IL

People's Pets

Gabrielle, Laura, Danielle, and Lisa each have a different pet. The pets are a puppy, a kitten, a horse, and a ferret. The names of the pets are Sarah, Dot, Raja, and Twinky. Try to find out who owns which pet and the pets' names using the clues below.

1. The kitten's name does not start with a letter that is made by two curves.
2. Lisa is allergic to furry animals.
3. The horse's name does not start with letters D-R.
4. The horse's name is not Twinky.
5. Danielle cannot have a horse because her brother might hurt himself, or a puppy because he has allergies.
6. Danielle does not have a kitten.
7. Twinky doesn't get out much.
8. Raja kneads her claws often.
9. Gabrielle's sister is scared of animals who usually grow large.
10. Laura's favorite movie is *101 Dalmatians*.

	Lisa	Danielle	Laura	Gabrielle	Twinky	Dot	Raja	Sarah
Kitten								
Horse								
Ferret								
Puppy								

Danielle Molisee
Gardnerville, NV

55

Winter
Word Search

Find the words below in the puzzle. Words may be up, down, across, backward, or diagonal.

```
S X D B M O N F R E E Z E E Q O O W A S
N R P L H E A D B A N D W R Y T S Z B N
O C W R I C E F I S H I N G U D H V I O
W J K A I J A H Q F P L O H F R O S T W
B X H S N O W G S I L F O N K S N M J S
A F G N O T H L S C A R F S B E K A K U
L B O O T S I I B E Y F J C N V M I V I
L X M W D D T H L I H A T N C O L D N T
S Y L F E B E M I T T E N S P L W Y V X
Z K D O W N H I L L S K I I N G U M Y Z
I J J R K S K A T E C A G Y E W Z S A O
W I N T E R Z V I C I C L E N V Q E P N
H F G R T B E C B D S N O W F L A K E S
G S N O W M O B I L E D O C D D G Z F E
```

SNOW, WINTER, COLD, WHITE, HAT, PLAY, SNOWBALLS, SNOW-
FORT, SNOWSUIT, ICE, SLIDE, SKI, ICE FISHING, SNOWMOBILE,
SKATE, BOOTS, MITTENS, SCARF, HEADBAND, SNOWMAN,
GLOVES, SNOWFLAKES, ICICLE, DOWNHILL SKIING, IGLOO,
FROST, FREEZE

Greg All
Menasha, WI

Brain Boggler

My fourth letter is in arm, but not in am.
My first letter is in care, but not in are.
My third letter is in dare, but not in red.
My last letter is in mare, but not in are.
My second letter is in hour, but not in our.
What am I?

Megan Harrell
Midland, TX

You're Invited to Join a World of Creativity!

Here's how to get published in *Creative Kids Magazine—The National Voice for Kids*

Creative Kids Guidelines

Creative Kids is a magazine filled with stories, poetry, games, puzzles, photography, and opinion by and for kids ages 8-14.

Follow all guidelines when submitting work. The editors cannot review or respond to materials that are improperly submitted. Improper submissions will not be retained.

Creative Kids is looking for the very best material by children (ages 8-14).

Please do not send school assignments. Send original work that you have completed on your own. Only authors may submit work (no teacher or parent submissions).

If a child's work is accepted, he or she will receive a free copy of the issue in which his or her work appears.

Submission Requirements Checklist

❑ Only the author, photographer, or artist may submit work.

❑ Work may include cartoons, songs, stories between 800 and 900 words, puzzles, photographs, artwork, games, activities, editorials, and plays.

❑ Include a separate cover page with each submission. Put your name, birthday, grade, school, and home address on this page.

❑ Send each submission in its own envelope via first class mail. *Do not send more than one submission per envelope.*

❑ Include a self-addressed, stamped, business-size envelope with each submission. *Do not seal your SASE.*

❑ Carefully proofread all submissions.

❑ All material must be typed on $8\frac{1}{2}$ x 11-inch white paper. Include your name at the top of each page.

❑ Send answers to games and puzzles.

❑ Keep a copy of all work submitted. When sending artwork, send a copy of the material. We will solicit the original work if it is accepted for publication.

❑ Mail submissions to Submissions Editor, *Creative Kids*, P.O. Box 8813, Waco, TX

Answers

Number Puzzle, Page 3

3	3	5	5	5
5	5	5	3	3
5	3	3	5	5
3	5	5	5	3
5	5	3	3	5

This is one solution. Answers may vary.

Brain Boggler, Page 3

dolphin

Galaxy Game, Page 4

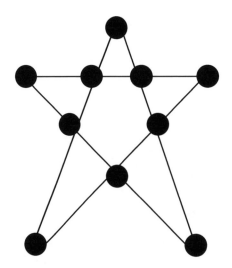

Chain Link, Page 4

1. volcano; 2. North; 3. throne; 4. new; 5. ewe; 6. weather; 7. erase; 8. seas; 9. ask; 10. skateboard

Making Connections, Page 5

1. bath; 2. water; 3. pop; 4. ice; 5. room; 6. rain; 7. ball; 8. dryer; 9. door; 10. man

Hidden Places, Page 5

1. When we went hiking, we took a m**ug and a** backpack.
2. A lar**ge or gia**nt animal was the least of our worries.
3. We saw a **cub a**nd a turtle on our trip.
4. Leopards are scarce, but that kind of ani**mal, I** have seen before.
5. Is that **guy an a**nimal?
6. Tom**'s pain** in his back prevented him from going to the woods.
7. We went to the bea**ch in a** boat.
8. We were **washing ton**s of clothes when we returned from the beach.
9. **In Dia**na's car, I found the keys that we thought were lost.
or
9. **In Diana**'s car, I found the keys that we thought were lost.

Pictures Worth A Thousand Words, Page 6

1. lost in the forest; 2. showcase; 3. backdraft; 4. broken pieces; 5. eye shadow; 6. read between the lines; 7. two peas in a pod; 8. back to the future; 9. spring forward, fall back

Brain Boggler, Page 7

The girl's birthday is December 31.

Scrambled States, Page 8

1. Arkansas; 2. Pennsylvania; 3. Rhode Island

On the Job, Page 9

Brenda: Nebori, *Life*, *Home Alone*, cookies; Jennifer: Davis, *Clue*, *Secret Garden*, candy bar; Laura: Dunhi, *Sorry!*, *Beauty and the Beast*, popcorn; Rachel: Alrich, *Aggravation*, *Aladdin*, peanuts; Emily: Saphin, checkers, *Sleepless in Seattle*, chips

Fictionaries, Page 10

1. Brrcussion; 2. Sleepdog; 3. Spams; Quackers; 4. Sootball; Cheferee

Brain Boggler, Page 10

They were two of a set of triplets. The third boy was never mentioned.

Sports Word Search, Page 11

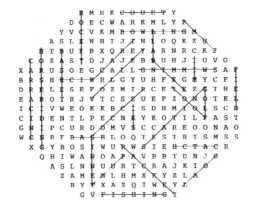

Brain Boggler, Page 11

A pestimation

United States Maze, Page 12

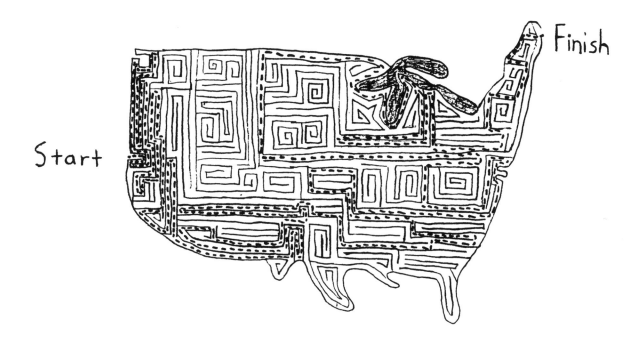

Dr. Seuss Crossword, Page 13

Across: 3. *You're Only Old Once*; 5. illustrator; 6. fiction; 7. Academy Awards; 9. *And To Think I Saw It On Mulberry St.*; 12. *Daisy-Head Mayzie*; 14. Grinch; 16. Theodore Geisel;
Down: 1. famous; 2. World War Two; 4. *The Cat in the Hat*; 8. World War One; 10. happy; 11. writer; 13. magazine; 14. glasses; 15. *ABC Book*; 17. Seuss

Clock Puzzle, Page 14

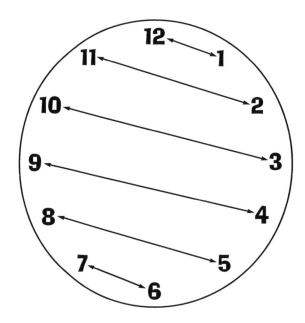

Friendly Code, Page 15

Treat others the way that you would like to be treated!

Puzzled About Writing, Page 16

Across: 2. verb; 7. pencil; 9. caption; 11. quote; 12. indent; 15. narrative; 16. noun; **Down:** 1. paper; 3. exclamation; 4. comma; 5. colon; 6. capitalize; 8. computer; 9. conjunction; 10. punctuation; 13. dictionary; 14. typewriter

Making Monsters, Page 17

Dr. Drathimer: Wachen; Dr. Fariche: Fariche Monster; Dr. Duehicel: Zart; Dr. Nartor: Trassey

Chain Reaction, Page 18

1. countdown; 2. downhill; 3. hillside; 4. sideshow; 5. showcase;
6. casework; 7. workshop; 8. shopworn; 9. worn-out; 10. outfield;
11. fieldstone; 12. stoneware; 13. warehouse; 14. housefly; 15. flywheel; 16. wheelchair; 17. chairlift; 18. liftoff

Brain Boggler, Page 18

Your lap

Hinky Pinkies, Page 19

1. bad dad; 2. round hound; 3. cool mule; 4. drunk skunk; 5. great bait; 6. teenie weenie; 7. shy guy; 8. scary berry; 9. gold mold;
10. crocodile smile; 11. mean bean; 12. sweet meat; 13. great date;
14. dog pog; 15. fake shake

Brain Boggler, Page 19

7735 = SELL

Pictures Worth a Thousand Words, Page 20

1. hair cut; 2. all for one and one for all; 3. Hollywood;
4. seven wonders of the world; 5. rock around the clock;
6. reincarnation

Brain Boggler, Page 20

A mutterance

School Days Word Search, Page 21

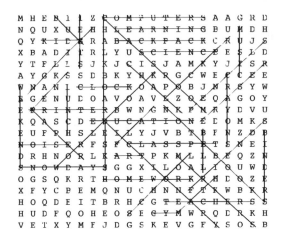

Hidden Animals, Page 22

1. Toba**cco wi**ll cause cancer.
2. Fi**fi sh**ied away from the other dog.
3. Mom likes to rea**d eer**ie books.
4. The man's business was called, Lem**mon Key**s & Locks.
5. If the pum**p ig**nites, will it explode?
6. Did you win at the c**lam b**ake?
7. Joey Sch**moo se**verely injured his arm when he fell.
8. May**be Ar**thur would like a piece of cake.

Chain Link, Page 22

1. purple; 2. lettuce; 3. center; 4. erosion; 5. onion; 6. once; 7. central; 8. Alex; 9. extra; 10. rattle

Where in the World?, Page 23

1.Canada; 2. USA; 3. Disney World

Man Maze, Page 24

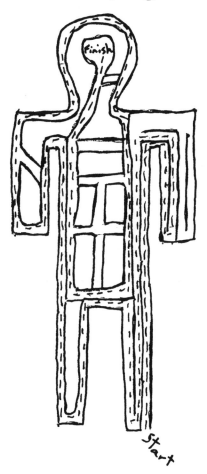

Brain Boggler, Page 24

Dark

Making Connections, Page 25

1. ground; 2. head; 3. neck; 4. air; 5. hair; 6. ship; 7. land; 8. court; 9. house; 10. hand; 11. bed; 12. pool; 13. super; 14. over; 15. ball; 16. light; 17. table; 18. board; 19. moon; 20. knee

Brain Boggler, Page 25

A harena

The Great Bike Race, Page 26

First: Diane, #6, green; second: Ed, #5, white; third: Amy, #2, red; fourth: Sean, #1, yellow; fifth: Mark, #3, blue; sixth: Julia, #4, black

Brain Boggler, Page 26

A rattorney

Pig Trivia, Page 27

Pigs weigh around 2 pounds at birth. The average weight of a full grown pig is 250 to 500 pounds. Pigs eat peanuts, fish, and meat scraps. In fact, pigs eat almost anything. Pigs are thought of as dirty, but they are actually very clean and make great pets.

Volleyball Word Search, Page 28

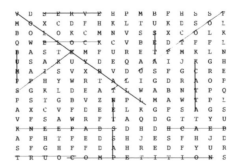

Brain Boggler, Page 28

The letter "T"

Concealed Fruit, Page 29

1. Could you give me my c**ap, ple**ase?
2. Pa**pa, pay a** dollar to the milkman.
3. "Make the ho**g rap!" E**instein said.
4. The big dog Fid**o ran ge**ntly toward the fence.
5. The **pea ch**anged color during the summer.
6. Play the tu**ba, Nan, a**s loud as you can.

Hinky Pinkies, Page 29

1. kitten's mittens; 2. dragon wagon; 3. fake rake;
4. fly pie; 5. flea tea; 6. quiet riot; 7. ferret's carrots; 8. cow chow; 9. funky monkey; 10. worm squirm; 11. large barge; 12. relevant elephant;
13. bear hair; 14. absurd bird; 15. tall mall

Authors & Movie Stars Crossword, Page 30

Across: 1. Red Riding Hood; 4. Michael Crichton; 5. Sheila Black;
6. Avi; 7. Dan Akroyd; 10. Steven Spielberg; 12. Jack Nicholson;
13. William Shatner; 14. Sally Field; **Down:** 2. Harrison Ford;
3. Robin Williams; 5. Steven Spielberg; 8. Frank Dixon; 9. R.L. Stine;
11. Tom Hanks

Dream Team I Word Search, Page 31

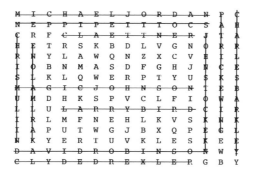

Brain Boggler, Page 31

Sports

Pictures Worth A Thousand Words, Page 32

1. go under the knife; 2. all worked up; 3. man in the moon; 4. one track mind; 5. traffic jam; 6. fender bender; 7. a small world after all; 8. split personality; 9. big deal

Pastimes, Page 33

1. movies; 2. bicycling; 3. rafting; 4. horseback riding; 5. volleyball; 6. hockey; 7. drawing; 8. hiking; 9. painting; 10. dance; 11. skating; 12. fishing; 13. video games; 14. reading; 15. gymnastics; 16. music
Message: My favorite things

Chain Link, Page 33

1. Earth; 2. thermometer; 3. error; 4. orange; 5. Germany; 6. nylon; 7. one; 8. needle; 9. lead; 10. advise

Magic Squares, Page 34

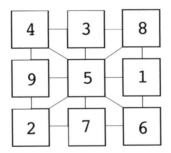

This is one solution. Answers may vary.

Brain Boggler, Page 34

Life

Movie Titles Crossword, Page 35

Across: 1. *Speed*; 4. *Alice in Wonderland*; 6. *Little Women*; 10. *Big*; 11. *Mask*; 12. *Dirty Dancing*; 13. *Home Alone*; **Down**: 2. *Philadelphia*; 3. *Forrest Gump*; 5. *E.T.*; 7. *The Fugitive*; 8. *Naked Gun*; 9. *Dumbo*

Hidden Names, Page 36

1. **John's on** the phone, do you want to talk to him?
2. The man's name is Ma**jor Dan** Jones.
3. Stop **kidd**ing around, Fred.
4. **One Al**ka-Seltzer, please.
5. Why doesn't the dog **bark, Ley**a?

Chain Link, Page 36

1. the; 2. head; 3. addition; 4. one; 5. neat; 6. ate; 7. teeth; 8. throw; 9. owe; 10. weep

Sports Match, Page 37

Andy Parker, tennis; Michelle Jones, baseball; Tori Smith, basketball; Jamie Giddens, football; Leslie Moore, cheerleader

Brain Boggler, Page 37

A smelody

Crazy Maze, Page 38

Picture Graph, Page 39

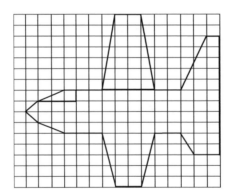

Eagle Trivia, Page 40

Bald eagles used to live all over the United States except in Texas. On the edge of extinction by hunters, they now live mainly in Alaska. Their main food is fish, but they also like to eat Snowshoe hare. Bald eagles have the best eyesight in the entire animal kingdom.

Making Connections, Page 41

1. teeth; 2. bar; 3. fly; 4. book; 5. up; 6. bed; 7. door; 8. tape; 9. breath;
10. walk; 11. clear; 12. hands; 13. fairy; 14. air; 15. neck; 16. heart;
17. rain; 18. guide; 19. iron; 20. cuff; 21. reel; 22. fan; 23. coin; 24. class;
25. fish

Civil War Word Search, Page 43

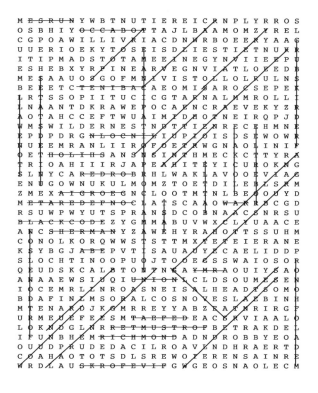

History Revealed, Page 44

Ellen: American Revolution, Mrs. Winston, fictional story, $2^{1}/_{2}$ pages; Sara: Declaration of Independence, Mrs. Crips, poem, 16 lines; Debra: World War II, Ms. Criston, research paper, 3 pages; Lisa: Constitution, Mrs. Prally, letter, 500 words

Picture Graph, Page 45

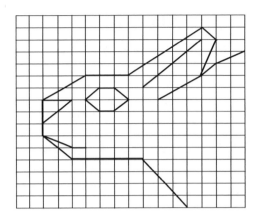

Tutankhamen Crossword, Page 47

Across: 2. arid; 4. hieroglyphics; 6. Tutankhamen; 9. coronation; 10. Khai; 12. burial chamber; 16. sand; 18. Egypt; 21. tomb; 23. Nile; 24. sphinx; 26. pyramid; **Down:** 1. sandals; 3. Carter; 5. sarcophagus; 7. goddess; 8. chariot; 11. gold; 13. alabaster; 14. curse; 15. ay; 17. Anubis; 19. pharaoh; 20. lion; 22. mummy; 25. XVIII

Pictures Worth A Thousand Words, Page 48

1. sandbox; 2. broken up; 3. red underwear; 4. touchdown; 5. time out; 6. airline; 7. in between; 8. happy meal; 9. bicycle; 10. upside down; 11. split second; 12. fourth grade

Brain Boggler, Page 48

A two-knee (tuna) fish

Chain Link, Page 49

1. umbrella; 2. lane; 3. Nebraska; 4. kale; 5. leave; 6. vermin; 7. invoke; 8. ketchup; 9. upset; 10. ether; 11. erase; 12. seven; 13. English; 14. shout; 15. Utah; 16. ahead; 17. advanced; 18. edit; 19. item; 20. emery

Brain Boggler, Page 49

Benjamin Franklin

Making Connections, Page 50

1. care; 2. snake; 3. bee; 4. aid; 5. bean; 6. water;
7. stone; 8. bond; 9. sled; 10. mat

Scrambled Phrases, Page 50

1. Every cloud has a silver lining. 2. A bird in the hand is
worth two in the bush. 3. A stitch in time saves nine. 4.
Don't look a gift horse in the mouth. 5. Don't bite the hand
that feeds you. 6. Everything that can go wrong will. 7.
Raining cats and dogs. 8. Here today gone tomorrow. 9.
Share and share alike. 10. Grin and bear it.

Yummy Word Search, Page 51

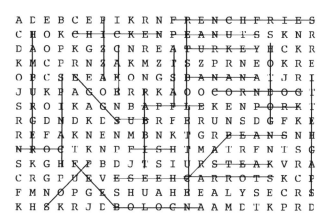

Brain Boggler, Page 51

They have bear feet.

Brain Boggler, Page 56

Babe Ruth

Horse Sense Crossword, Page 57

Across: 3. stall; 4. pony; 5. stallion; 7. horse; 10. mare; 11. bronco; 13. horseback riding; 15. saddle; 16. rider; 19. horseracing; **Down:** 1. gallop; 2. horseshoe; 6. trot; 8. mount; 9. jockey; 10. mustang; 12. foal; 14. Arabian; 17. reins; 18. stirrup

Number Puzzler, Page 58

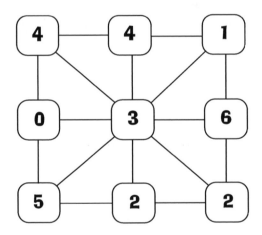

This is one solution. Answers may vary.

People's Pets, Page 59

Lisa: horse, Sarah; Danielle: ferret, Twinky; Laura: puppy, Dot; Gabrielle: kitten, Raja

Winter Word Search, Page 60

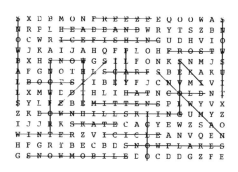

Brain Boggler, Page 60

Charm